100
Hadiths for Kids Ages 10-12
(From the Book of Al-Bukhari)

100
Hadiths for Kids Ages 10-12

(From the Book of Al-Bukhari)

Dedication

'(Our Lord! Accept this from us. You are the All-Hearing, the All-Knowing).'

(The Qur'aan: Chapter 2, Verse 127)

Hadith from the Book of Revelation:

1. Narrated by Ibn 'Abbaas (ra):

"Prophet Muhammad (PBUH) was the most generous of all the people, and he used to reach the peak in generosity in the month of Ramadhaan when Jibreel (AS) met him. Jibreel used to meet him every night of Ramadhaan to teach him the Qur'aan. Prophet Muhammad (PBUH) was the most generous person, even more generous than the strong uncontrollable wind (in readiness and haste to do charitable deeds)."

Hadiths from the Book of Belief:

2. Narrated by 'Aishah (ra):

Whenever Prophet Muhammad (PBUH) ordered the Muslims to do something, he used to order them deeds which were easy for them to do, (according to their strength and endurance).
They said, "O Prophet Muhammad (PBUH)! We are not like you. Allaah has forgiven your past and future sins."
So Prophet Muhammad (PBUH) became angry and it was apparent on his face. He said, "I am the most God-fearing, and know Allaah better than all of you do."

3. Narrated by Abu Sa'eed Al-Khudri (ra): The Prophet Muhammad (PBUH) said,

"When the people of Paradise will enter Paradise and the people of Hell will go to Hell, Allaah will order those who have had faith equal to the weight of a grain of a mustard seed to be taken out from Hell. So they will be taken out but (by then) they will be blackened (charred). Then they will be put in the river of *Haya'* (rain) or *Hayat* (life) (the Narrator is in doubt as to which is the right term), and they will revive like a grain that grows near the bank of a flood channel. Don't you see that it comes out yellow and twisted."

4. Narrated by Abu Hurayrah (ra): Prophet Muhammad (PBUH) was asked,

"What is the best deed?"
He replied, "To believe in Allaah and His Apostle (Muhammad)."
The questioner then asked, "What is the next (in goodness)?"
He replied, "To participate in Jihad in Allaah's Cause."
The questioner again asked, "What is the next (in goodness)?"
He replied, "To perform Hajj (Pilgrimage to Makkah) Mabroor, (which is accepted by Allaah and is performed with the intention of seeking Allaah's Pleasure only, and not to show off, without committing a sin, and in accordance with the traditions of the Prophet)."

5. Narrated by Ibn 'Abbaas (ra): The Prophet Muhammad (PBUH)said:

"I was shown the Hell-fire and the majority of its dwellers were women who were ungrateful."
It was asked, "Do they disbelieve in Allaah?" (or are they ungrateful to Allaah?)
He replied, "They are ungrateful to their husbands and are ungrateful for the favors and the good (charitable deeds) done to them. If you have always been good (benevolent) to one of them and then she sees something in you (not of her liking), she will say, 'I have never received any good from you.'"

6. Narrated by Al-Ma'rur (ra): At Ar-Rabadha I met Abu Dharr who was wearing a cloak, and his slave, too, was wearing a similar one. I asked about the reason for it. He replied,

"I abused a person by calling his mother with bad names. The Prophet said to me, 'O Abu Dharr! Did you abuse him by calling his mother with bad names? You still have some characteristics of ignorance. Your slaves are your brothers and Allaah has put them under your command. So whoever has a brother under his command should feed him of what he eats and dress him of what he wears. Do not ask them (slaves) to do things beyond their capacity (power) and if you do so, then help them.'"

7. Narrated by Al-Ahnaf bin Qais (ra): While I was going to help this man ('Ali Ibn Abi Talib), Abu Bakra met me and asked,

"Where are you going?"
I replied, "I am going to help that person."
He said, "Go back for I have heard Prophet Muhammad (PBUH) saying, 'When two Muslims fight (meet) each other with their swords, both the murderer as well as the murdered will go to the Hell-fire.'
I said, 'O Prophet Muhammad (PBUH)! It is all right for the murderer but what about the murdered one?'
Prophet Muhammad (PBUH) replied, 'He surely had the intention to kill his companion.'"

8. Narrated by 'Abdullaah bin 'Amr (ra): The Prophet Muhammad (PBUH) said,

"Whoever has the following four (characteristics) will be a pure hypocrite and whoever has one of the following four characteristics will have one characteristic of hypocrisy unless and until he gives it up.
1. Whenever he is entrusted, he betrays.
2. Whenever he speaks, he tells a lie.
3. Whenever he makes a covenant, he proves treacherous.
4. Whenever he quarrels, he behaves in a very imprudent, evil and insulting manner."

9. Narrated by Abu Hurayrah (ra): The Prophet Muhammad (PBUH) said,

"Religion is very easy and whoever overburdens himself in his religion will not be able to continue in that way. So you should not be extremists, but try to be near to perfection and receive the good tidings that you will be rewarded; and gain strength by worshiping in the mornings, and the nights."

10. Narrated by 'Aishah (ra): Once the Prophet Muhammad (PBUH) came while a woman was sitting with me,

He said, "Who is she?"
I replied, "She is so and so," and told him about her (excessive) praying.
He said disapprovingly, "Do (good) deeds which are within your capacity (without being overtaxed) as Allaah does not get tired (of giving rewards) but (surely) you will get tired and the best deed (act of worship) in the sight of Allaah is that which is done regularly."

11. Narrated by Anas (ra): The Prophet Muhammad (PBUH) said,

"Whoever says, 'None has the right to be worshiped but Allaah' and has in his heart good (faith) equal to the weight of a barley grain will be taken out of Hell. And whoever says, 'None has the right to be worshiped but Allaah and has in his heart good (faith) equal to the weight of a wheat grain will be taken out of Hell. And whoever says, 'None has the right to be worshiped but Allaah and has in his heart good (faith) equal to the weight of an atom will be taken out of Hell."

12. Narrated by 'Umar bin Al-Khattaab (ra): Once a Jew said to me,

"O the Chief of believers! There is a verse in your Holy Book which is read by all of you (Muslims), and had it been revealed to us, we would have taken that day (on which it was revealed as a day of celebration."
'Umar bin Al-Khattaab asked, "Which is that verse?"
The Jew replied, *"This day I have perfected your religion for you, completed My favor upon you, and have chosen for you Islaam as your religion."* (5: 3)
'Umar replied, "No doubt, we know when and where this verse was revealed to the Prophet. It was Friday and the Prophet was standing at 'Arafaat (i.e., the Day of Hajj)."

13. Narrated by Talhah bin 'Ubaydullaah (ra): A man from Najd with unkempt hair came to Prophet Muhammad (PBUH) and we heard his loud voice but could not understand what he was saying; till he came near and then we came to know that he was asking about Islaam.

Prophet Muhammad (PBUH) said, "You have to offer prayers perfectly five times in a day and night (24 hours)." The man asked, "Is there any more (praying)?" Prophet Muhammad (PBUH) replied, "No, but if you want to offer the *nawaafil* prayers (you can)." Prophet Muhammad (PBUH) further said to him: "You have to observe fasts during the month of Ramadhaan." The man asked, "Is there any more fasting?" Prophet Muhammad (PBUH) replied, "No, but if you want to observe the *nawaafil* fasts (you can)." Then Prophet Muhammad (PBUH) further said to him, "You have to pay the Zakat (obligatory charity)." The man asked, "Is there any thing other than the Zakat for me to pay?" Prophet Muhammad (PBUH) replied, "No, unless you want to give alms of your own."
And then that man retreated saying, "By Allaah! I will neither do less nor more than this."
Prophet Muhammad (PBUH) said, "If what he said is true, then he will be successful (i.e., he will be granted Paradise)."

14. Narrated by Abu Hurayrah (ra): Prophet Muhammad (PBUH) said,

"(A believer) who accompanies the funeral procession of a Muslim out of sincere faith and hoping to attain Allaah's reward and remains with it till the funeral prayer is offered and the burial ceremonies are over, he will return with a reward of two *qiraats*. Each *qiraat* is like the size of the (Mount) Uhud. He who offers the funeral prayer only and returns before the burial, will return with the reward of one *qiraat* only."

15. Narrated by 'Umar bin Al-Khattaab (ra): Prophet Muhammad (PBUH) said,

"The reward of deeds depends upon the intention, and every person will get the reward according to what he has intended. So whoever emigrated for Allaah and His Apostle, then his emigration was for Allaah and His Apostle. And whoever emigrated for worldly benefits or to marry a woman, his emigration was for what he emigrated for."

Hadiths from the Book of Knowledge:

16. Narrated by Abu Wail (ra): 'Abdullaah used to give a religious talk to the people on every Thursday. Once a man said,

"O Aba 'Abdur-Rahmaan! (By Allaah) I wish if you could preach us daily."
He replied, "The only thing which prevents me from doing so, is that I hate to bore you, and no doubt I take care of you in preaching by selecting a suitable time just as the Prophet used to do with us, for fear of making us bored."

17. Narrated by 'Abdullaah bin Mas'ood (ra): The Prophet Muhammad (PBUH) said,

"Do not wish to be like anyone except in two cases. (The first is) A person, whom Allaah has given wealth and he spends it righteously; (the second is) the one whom Allaah has given wisdom (the Holy Qur'aan) and he acts according to it and teaches it to others."

18. Narrated by Mu'awiyah (ra): I heard Prophet Muhammad (PBUH) saying,

"If Allaah wants to do good to a person, He makes him comprehend the Religion. I am just a distributor, but the grant is from Allaah. (And remember) that this nation (true Muslims) will keep on following Allaah's teachings strictly and they will not be harmed by any one going on a different path till Allaah's order (Day of Judgment) is established."

19. Narrated by Ibn 'Umar (ra): Prophet Muhammad (PBUH) said,

"While I was sleeping, I saw that a cup full of milk was brought to me and I drank my fill till I noticed (the milk) its wetness coming out of my nails. Then I gave the remaining milk to 'Umar Ibn Al-Khattaab."
The Companions of the Prophet asked, "What have you interpreted (about this dream), O Prophet Muhammad (PBUH)?"
He replied, "(It is religious) knowledge."

20. Narrated by Abu Hurayrah (ra): The Prophet Muhammad (PBUH) said,

"(Religious) knowledge will be taken away (by the death of religious scholars), ignorance (in religion) and afflictions will appear; and *harj* will increase."
It was asked, "What is *harj*, O Prophet Muhammad (PBUH)?"
He replied by beckoning with his hand indicating "killing."

21. Narrated by 'Abdullaah bin Abi Mulaika (ra): 'Uqba bin Al-Harith said that he had married the daughter of Abi Ihab bin 'Aziz. Later on a woman came to him and said,

"I have suckled (nursed) 'Uqba and the woman whom he married (his wife) at my breast." 'Uqba said to her, "Neither I knew that you have suckled (nursed) me nor did you tell me." Then he rode over to see Prophet Muhammad (PBUH) at Medina, and asked him about it. Prophet Muhammad (PBUH) said, "How can you keep her as a wife when it has been said (that she is your foster-sister)?" Then 'Uqba divorced her, and she married another man.

22. Narrated by Abu Mas'ood Al-Ansaari (ra): Once a man said to Prophet Muhammad (PBUH),

"O Prophet Muhammad (PBUH)! I may not attend the (compulsory congregational) prayer because so and so (the Imam) prolongs the prayer when he leads us for it. The narrator added: "I never saw the Prophet more furious in giving advice than he was on that day. The Prophet said, 'O people! Some of you make others dislike good deeds (the prayers). So whoever leads the people in prayer should shorten it because among them there are the sick, the weak and the needy (having some jobs to do).'"

23. Narrated by Abu Burda's father: Prophet Muhammad (PBUH) said,

"Three persons will have a double reward:
1. A person from the people of the scriptures who believed in his prophet (Jesus or Moses) and then believed in the Prophet Muhammad (i.e., has embraced Islaam).
2. A slave who discharges his duties to Allaah and his master.
3. The master of a female-slave, who teaches her good manners and educates her in the best possible way (the religion), then manumits her and marries her."

24. Narrated by Ibn 'Abbaas (ra): Once Prophet Muhammad (PBUH) came out while Bilaal (ra) was accompanying him.

He went towards the women thinking that they had not heard him (i.e., his sermon). So he preached to them and ordered them to pay alms. (Hearing that) the women started giving alms; some donated their earrings, some gave their rings and Bilaal was collecting them in the corner of his garment.

25. Narrated by Abu Sa'eed Al-Khudri (ra):

Some women requested for the Prophet to fix a day for them as the men were taking all his time. On that he promised them one day for religious lessons and commandments. Once during such a lesson the Prophet (PBUH) said, "A woman whose three children die will be shielded by them from the Hell fire."
On that a woman asked, "If only two die?"
He replied, "Even two (will shield her from the Hell-fire)."

26. Narrated by Anas (ra):

The fact which stops me from narrating a great number of hadiths to you is that the Prophet (PBUH) said: "Whoever tells a lie against me intentionally, then (surely) let him occupy his seat in the Hell-fire."

27. Narrated by Abu Hurayrah (ra): The Prophet Muhammad (PBUH) said,

"Name yourselves with my name (use my name) but do not name yourselves with my *kunya* name (i.e., Abu-l Qasim). And whoever sees me in a dream then surely he has seen me for Satan cannot impersonate me. And whoever tells a lie against me (intentionally), then (surely) let him occupy his seat in the Hell-fire."

28. Narrated by Umm Salamah (ra):

One night Prophet Muhammad (PBUH) got up and said, "SubhaanAllaah! How many afflictions have been descended tonight and how many treasures have been disclosed! Go and wake the sleeping lady occupants of these dwellings (his wives) up (for prayers). A well-dressed (soul) in this world may be naked in the Hereafter."

29. Narrated by 'Abdullaah bin 'Umar (ra):

Once the Prophet led us in the 'Isha prayer during the last days of his life and after finishing it (the prayer) (with *tasleem*) he said: "Do you realize (the importance of) this night? Nobody present on the surface of the earth tonight will be living after the completion of one hundred years from this night."

30. Narrated by Abu Hurayrah (ra):

I said to Prophet Muhammad (PBUH), "I hear many narrations (hadiths) from you but I forget them."
Prophet Muhammad (PBUH) said, "Spread your *rida'* (garment)."
I did accordingly and then he moved his hands as if filling them with something (and emptied them in my *rida*) and then said, "Take and wrap this sheet over your body." I did it and after that I never forgot any thing.

31. Narrated by Jarir (ra):

The Prophet (PBUH) said to me during Hajjat-al-Wida': Let the people keep quiet and listen. Then he said (addressing the people), "Do not (become infidels) revert to disbelief after me by striking the necks (cutting the throats) of one another (killing each other)."

32. Narrated by Aswad (ra): Ibn Az-Zubair said to me,

"'Aishah used to tell you secretly a number of things. What did she tell you about the Ka'bah?" I replied, "She told me that once the Prophet said, 'O 'Aisha! Had not your people been still close to the pre-Islamic period of ignorance (infidelity)! I would have dismantled the Ka'bah and would have made two doors in it; one for entrance and the other for exit.'" Later on Ibn Az-Zubair did the same.

33. Narrated by Ibn 'Umar (ra): A man asked the Prophet Muhammad (PBUH):

"What (kinds of clothes) should a Muhrim (a Muslim intending to perform 'Umrah or Hajj) wear?"
He replied, "He should not wear a shirt, a turban, trousers, a head cloak or garment scented with saffron or *wars* (kinds of perfumes). And if he has no slippers, then he can use *khuffs* (leather socks), but the socks should be cut short so as to make the ankles bare."

Hadiths from the Book of Ablutions (Wudoo')

34. Narrated by Nu'am Al-Mujmir (ra):

Once I went up to the roof of the mosque, along with Abu Hurayrah. He performed ablution and said, "I heard the Prophet saying, 'On the Day of Resurrection, my followers will be called *"Al-Ghurr-ul-Muhajjalun"* from the trace of ablution, and whoever can increase the area of his radiance should do so (i.e., by performing ablution regularly).'"

35. Narrated by Abu Hurayrah (ra): The Prophet Muhammad (PBUH) said,

"If anyone of you performs ablution he should put water in his nose and then blow it out and whoever cleans his private parts with stones should do so with odd numbers. And whoever wakes up from his sleep should wash his hands before putting them in the water for ablution, because nobody knows where his hands were during sleep."

36. Narrated by Ibn Shihab (ra):

Mahmood bin Ar-Rabi', who was the person on whose face the Prophet (PBUH) had released a mouthful of water from his family's well while he was a boy, and 'Urwa (on the authority of Al-Miswar and others) who testified each other, said, "Whenever the Prophet performed ablution, his Companions were nearly fighting for the remains of the water."

37. Narrated by As-Sa'ib bin Yazid (ra):

My aunt took me to the Prophet (PBUH) and said, "O Prophet Muhammad (PBUH)! This son of my sister has got a disease in his legs." So he passed his hands on my head and prayed for Allaah's blessings for me; then he performed ablution and I drank from the remaining water.
I stood behind him and saw the seal of Prophethood between his shoulders, and it was like the *"zir-al-hijla"* (means the button of a small tent, but some said 'egg of a partridge').

38. Narrated by 'Aishah (ra): Prophet Muhammad (PBUH) said,

"If any one of you feels drowsy while praying he should go to bed (sleep) till his slumber is over, because in praying while drowsy one does not know whether one is asking for forgiveness or for a bad thing for oneself."

39. Narrated by 'Amr bin 'Amir (ra): Anas (ra) said,

"The Prophet (PBUH) used to perform ablution for every prayer."
I asked Anas, "What you used to do?"
Anas replied, "We used to pray with the same ablution until we break it with *hadath*."

40. Narrated by Maymoonah (ra): Prophet Muhammad (PBUH) was asked regarding ghee (cooking butter) in which a mouse had fallen,

He said, "Take out the mouse and throw away the ghee around it and use the rest."

41. Narrated by Abu Hurayrah (ra): Prophet Muhammad (PBUH) said,

"We (Muslims) are the last (people to come in the world) but (will be) the foremost (on the Day of Resurrection)."
The same narrator told that the Prophet had said, "You should not pass urine in stagnant water which is not flowing then (you may need to) wash in it."

Hadiths from the Book of Rubbing Hands and Feet with Dust (Tayammum)

42. Narrated by Jaabir bin 'Abdullaah (ra):

The Prophet (PBUH) said, "I have been given five things which were not given to any one else before me.

1. Allaah made me victorious by awe (by His frightening my enemies) for a distance of one month's journey.

2. The earth has been made for me (and for my followers) a place for praying and a thing to perform *tayammum*; therefore anyone of my followers can pray wherever the time of a prayer is due.

3. The booty has been made *halaal* (lawful) for me yet it was not lawful for anyone else before me.

4. I have been given the right of intercession (on the Day of Resurrection).

5. Every Prophet used to be sent to his nation only but I have been sent to all mankind.

Hadiths from the Book of Prayers (Salaat)

43.   Narrated by Abu Hurayrah (ra):

The Prophet (PBUH) said, "None of you should offer prayer in a single garment that does not cover the shoulders."

44.   Narrated by 'Abdullaah bin 'Umar (ra):

Prophet Muhammad (PBUH) saw sputum on the wall of the mosque in the direction of the qiblah and scraped it off. He faced the people and said, "Whenever any one of you is praying, he should not spit in front of him because in the prayer Allaah is in front of him."

45.   Narrated by Abu Hurayrah (ra):

On the Day of Nahr (10th of Dhul-Hijjah, in the year prior to the last Hajj of the Prophet when Abu Bakr was the leader of the pilgrims in that Hajj), Abu Bakr sent me along with other announcers to Mina to make a public announcement: "No pagan is allowed to perform Hajj after this year and no naked person is allowed to perform the *tawaaf* around the Ka'bah. Then Prophet Muhammad (PBUH) sent 'Ali to read out the Soorat Bara'a (At-Taubah) to the people; so he made the announcement along with us on the day of Nahr in Mina: "No pagan is allowed to perform Hajj after this year and no naked person is allowed to perform the *tawaaf* around the Ka'bah."

46.   Narrated by 'Aishah (ra):

The Prophet (PBUH) said, "I was looking at its (*khamisa's*) marks during the prayers and I was afraid that it may put me in trial (by taking away my attention)."

47. Narrated by Ibn 'Abbaas (ra):

When the Prophet (PBUH) entered the Ka'bah, he invoked Allaah in each and every side of it and did not pray till he came out of it, and offered a two-*rakaat* prayer facing the Ka'bah and said, "This is the qiblah."

48. Narrated by Jaabir (ra):

Prophet Muhammad (PBUH) used to pray (optional, non-obligatory prayer) while riding on his mount (Rahila) wherever it turned, and whenever he wanted to pray the compulsory prayer he dismounted and prayed facing the qiblah.

49.   Narrated by 'Aishah (ra):

Umm Habibah and Umm Salamah mentioned about a church they had seen in Ethiopia in which there were pictures. They told the Prophet about it, on which he said, "If any religious man dies amongst those people they would build a place of worship at his grave and make these pictures in it. They will be the worst creature in the sight of Allaah on the Day of Resurrection."

50.   Narrated by 'Abdullaah bin 'Umar (ra):

Prophet Muhammad (PBUH) said, "Do not enter (the places) of these people where Allaah's punishment had fallen unless you do so weeping. If you do not weep, do not enter (the places of these people) because Allaah's curse and punishment which fell upon them may fall upon you."

51. Narrated by 'Aishah (ra) and 'Abdullaah bin 'Abbaas (ra):

When the last moment of the life of Prophet Muhammad (PBUH) came he started putting his *khamisa* on his face, and when he felt hot and short of breath he took it off his face and said, "May Allaah curse the Jews and Christians for they built the places of worship at the graves of their Prophets." The Prophet was warning (Muslims) of what those people had done.

52. Narrated by 'Aishah (ra):

When the verses of Soorat Al-Baqarah concerning usury (*riba*) were revealed, the Prophet (PBUH) went to the mosque and recited them in front of the people and then banned the trade of alcohol.

53. Narrated by Sahl bin Sa'd (ra):

Prophet Muhammad (PBUH) went to Fatimah's (ra) house but did not find 'Ali there. So he asked, "Where is your cousin?"
She replied, "There was something between us and he got angry with me and went out. He did not sleep (mid-day nap) in the house."
Prophet Muhammad (PBUH) asked a person to look for him. That person came and said, "O Prophet Muhammad (PBUH)! He (Ali) is sleeping in the mosque."
Prophet Muhammad (PBUH) went there and 'Ali was lying down. His upper body cover had fallen down to one side of his body and he was covered with dust. Prophet Muhammad (PBUH) started cleaning the dust from him saying: "Get up! O Aba Turab. Get up! O Aba Turab (literally means: O father of dust)."

54. Narrated by Naafi' (ra):

Ibn 'Umar (ra) said, "While the Prophet (PBUH) was on the pulpit, a man asked him how to offer the night prayers. He replied, 'Pray two *rakaat* at a time and then two and then two and so on, and if you are afraid of the dawn (the approach of the time of the Fajr prayer) pray one *rakaat* and that will be the *witr* for all the *rakaat* which you have offered."
Ibn 'Umar said, "The last *rakaat* of the night prayer should be odd for the Prophet ordered it to be so."

55. Narrated by Abu Hurayrah (ra):

Prophet Muhammad (PBUH) said, "The angels keep on asking Allaah's forgiveness for anyone of you, as long as he is at his *musalla* (praying place) and he does not pass wind (*hadath*). They say, 'O Allaah! Forgive him, O Allaah! Be merciful to him."

56. Narrated by Abu Hurayrah (ra):

The Prophet (PBUH) said, "The prayer offered in congregation is twenty five times more superior (in reward) to the prayer offered alone in one's house or in a business center, because if one performs ablution and does it perfectly, and then proceeds to the mosque with the sole intention of praying, then for each step which he takes towards the mosque, Allaah upgrades him a degree in reward and (forgives) crosses out one sin till he enters the mosque. When he enters the mosque he is considered in prayer as long as he is waiting for the prayer and the angels keep on asking for Allaah's forgiveness for him and they keep on saying: 'O Allaah! Be merciful to him, O Allaah! Forgive him', as long as he keeps on sitting at his praying place and does not pass wind."

Hadiths from the Book of Times of the Prayer

57. Narrated by Abu Hurayrah (ra):

I heard Prophet Muhammad (PBUH) saying, "If there was a river at the door of anyone of you and he took a bath in it five times a day would you notice any dirt on him?" They said, "Not a trace of dirt would be left." The Prophet added, "That is the example of the five prayers with which Allaah blots out (annuls) evil deeds."

58. Narrated by Anas (ra):

The Prophet (PBUH) said, "Do the prostration properly and do not put your forearms flat with elbows touching the ground like a dog. And if you want to spit, do not spit in front, nor to the right for the person in prayer is speaking in private to his Lord."

59. Narrated by Abu Al-Minhal (ra):

Abu Barza said, "The Prophet used to offer the Fajr (prayer) when one could recognize the person sitting by him (after the prayer) and he used to recite between 60 to 100 aayaat (verses) of the Qur'aan. He used to offer the Dhuhr prayer as soon as the sun declined (at noon) and the 'Asr at a time when a man might go and return from the farthest place in Madinah and find the sun still hot. (The sub-narrator forgot what was said about the Maghrib). He did not mind delaying the 'Isha prayer to one third of the night or the middle of the night."

60. Narrated by Qais (ra):

Jarir said, "We were with the Prophet and he looked at the moon--full-moon--and said, 'Certainly you will see your Lord as you see this moon and you will have no trouble in seeing Him. So if you can avoid missing (through sleep or business, etc.) a prayer before the sun-rise (Fajr) and a prayer before sunset ('Asr), you must do so.' He then recited Allaah's Statement: *'And celebrate the praises of your Lord before the rising of the sun, and before (its) setting."* (50: 39)
Isma'il said, "Offer those prayers and do not miss them."

61.   Narrated by Abu Hurayrah (ra):

Prophet Muhammad (PBUH) said, "Angels come to you in succession by night and day and all of them get together at the time of the Fajr and 'Asr prayers. Those who have passed the night with you (or stayed with you) ascend (to the Heaven) and Allaah asks them, though He knows everything about you, well, 'In what state did you leave my slaves?' The angels reply: 'When we left them they were praying and when we reached them, they were praying.'"

62.   Narrated by Abdullaah (ra):

"One night Prophet Muhammad (PBUH) led us in the 'Isha' prayer and that is the one called Al-'Atma by the people. After the completion of the prayer, he faced us and said, 'Do you know the importance of this night? Nobody present on the surface of the earth to-night will be living after one hundred years from this night.'"

63. Narrated by Muhammad bin 'Amr (ra):

We asked Jaabir bin 'Abdullaah about the prayers of the Prophet. He said, "He used to pray Dhuhr prayer at mid-day, the 'Asr when the sun was still hot, and the Maghrib after sunset (at its stated time). The 'Isha was offered early if the people gathered, and used to be delayed if their number was less; and the morning prayer was offered when it was still dark."

64. Narrated by 'Aishah (ra):

The believing women covered with their veiling sheets used to attend the Fajr prayer with Prophet Muhammad (PBUH), and after finishing the prayer they would return to their home and nobody could recognize them because of the darkness.

65.   Narrated by Abu Hurayrah (ra):

Prophet Muhammad (PBUH) forbade the offering of two prayers:
1. After the morning prayer till the sun rises.
2. After the 'Asr prayer till the sun sets.

66.   Narrated by Jaabir bin 'Abdullaah (ra):

On the Day of Al-Khandaq (the Battle of the Trench), 'Umar bin Al-Khattaab came cursing the disbelievers of Quraysh after the sun had set and said, "O Prophet Muhammad (PBUH) I could not offer the 'Asr prayer till the sun had set." The Prophet said, "By Allaah! I, too, have not prayed." So we turned towards Buthan, and the Prophet performed ablution and we too performed ablution and offered the 'Asr prayer after the sun had set, and then he offered the Maghrib prayer.

67. Narrated by Anas (ra):

The Prophet said, "If any one forgets a prayer he should pray that prayer when he remembers it. There is no expiation except to pray the same." Then he recited: *"Establish prayer for My (i.e., Allaah's) remembrance."* (20: 14)

Hadiths from the Book of Call to Prayers (Adhaan)

68.   Narrated by Ibn 'Umar (ra):

When the Muslims arrived at Madinah, they used to assemble for the prayer, and used to guess the time for it. During those days, the practice of Adhaan for the prayers had not been introduced yet. Once they discussed this problem regarding the call for prayer. Some people suggested the use of a bell like the Christians, others proposed a trumpet like the horn used by the Jews, but 'Umar was the first to suggest that a man should call (the people) for the prayer; so Prophet Muhammad (PBUH) ordered Bilaal to get up and pronounce the Adhaan for prayers.

69.   Narrated by Abu Hurayrah (ra):

Prophet Muhammad (PBUH) said, "When the Adhaan is pronounced Satan takes to his heels and passes wind with noise during his flight in order not to hear the Adhaan. When the Adhaan is completed he comes back and again takes to his heels when the *Iqaamah* is pronounced, and after its completion he returns again till he whispers into the heart of the person (to divert his attention from his prayer) and makes him remember things which he does not recall to his mind before the prayer; and that causes him to forget how much he has prayed."

70.   Narrated by Yahya as above (586) and added:

"Some of my companions told me that Hisham had said, 'When the Mu'adhdhin said, "Hayya alas-salaah (come for the prayer)." Mu'awiyah said, "Laa hawla wa laa quwwata illaa billaah (There is neither might nor any power except with Allaah)" and added, "We heard your Prophet saying the same.'"

71. Narrated by Abu Hurayrah (ra):

Prophet Muhammad (PBUH) said, "If the people knew the reward for pronouncing the Adhaan and for standing in the first row (in congregational prayers) and found no other way to get that except by drawing lots they would draw lots, and if they knew the reward of the Dhuhr prayer (in the early moments of its stated time) they would race for it (go early), and if they knew the reward of 'Isha and Fajr (morning) prayers in congregation, they would come to offer them even if they had to crawl."

72. Narrated by Anas bin Maalik (ra):

"When the Mu'adhdhin pronounced the Adhaan, some of the Companions of the Prophet would proceed to the pillars of the mosque (for the prayer) till the Prophet arrived; and in this way they used to pray two *rakaat* before the Maghrib prayer. There used to be a short time between the Adhaan and the Iqaamah." Shu'ba said, "There used to be a very short interval between the two (Adhaan and Iqaamah)."

73. Narrated by 'Abdullaah bin Abi Qatadah (ra):

My father said, "While we were praying with the Prophet he heard the noise of some people. After the prayer he said, 'What is the matter?' They replied, 'We were hurrying for the prayer.' He said, 'Do not make haste for the prayer, and whenever you come for the prayer, you should come with calmness, and pray whatever you get (with the people) and complete the rest which you have missed.'"

74. Narrated by Salim (ra):

I heard Umm Ad-Darda' saying, "Abu Ad-Darda' entered the house in an angry mood. I said to him, 'What makes you angry?' He replied, 'By Allaah! I do not find the followers of Muhammad doing those good things (which they used to do before) except the offering of congregational prayer.'" (This happened in the last days in the life of Abu Ad-Darda' during the rule of 'Uthmaan (ra)).

75.   Narrated by Abu Musa (ra):

The Prophet (PBUH) said, "The people who get tremendous reward for the prayer are those who are farthest away (from the mosque) and then those who are next farthest and so on. Similarly one who waits to pray with the Imam has greater reward than one who prays and goes to bed.

76.   Narrated by Abu Hurayrah (ra):

Prophet Muhammad (PBUH) said, "If the Imam leads the prayer correctly then he and you will receive the rewards but if he makes a mistake (in the prayer) then you will receive the reward for the prayer and the sin will be his."

77.   Narrated by Anas bin Maalik (ra):

I never prayed behind any Imam a prayer lighter and more perfect than that behind the Prophet; and he used to cut short the prayer whenever he heard the cries of a child lest he should put the child's mother to trial.

78. Narrated by Abu Mas'ood (ra):

A man came and said, "O Prophet Muhammad (PBUH)! By Allaah, I keep away from the morning prayer only because so and so prolongs the prayer when he leads us in it."
The narrator said, "I never saw Prophet Muhammad (PBUH) more furious in giving advice than he was at that time. He then said, 'Some of you make people dislike good deeds (the prayer). So whoever among you leads the people in prayer should shorten it because among them are the weak, the old and the needy.'"

79. Narrated by Abu Hurayrah (ra):

The Prophet (PBUH) said, "The Imam is to be followed. Say the *takbeer* when he says it; bow if he bows; if he says 'Sami a-l-laahu liman hamidah', say, ' Rabbanaa wa-laka-l-hamd'; prostrate if he prostrates and pray sitting altogether if he prays sitting."

Hadiths from the Book of Characteristics of Prayer

80. Narrated by 'Abdullaah bin 'Abbaas (ra):

A solar eclipse occurred during the lifetime of Prophet Muhammad (PBUH), so he offered the eclipse prayer. His Companions asked, "O Prophet Muhammad (PBUH)! We saw you trying to take something while standing at your place and then we saw you retreating." The Prophet (PBUH) said, "I was shown Paradise and wanted to have a bunch of fruit from it. Had I taken it, you would have eaten from it as long as the world remains."

81. Narrated by Anas bin Maalik (ra):

The Prophet (PBUH) said, "What is wrong with those people who look towards the sky during the prayer?" His talk grew stern while delivering this speech and he said, "They should stop (looking towards the sky during the prayer); otherwise their eye-sight would be taken away."

82. Narrated by Ibn 'Abbaas (ra):

The Prophet (PBUH) recited aloud in the prayers in which he was ordered to do so and quietly in the prayers in which he was ordered to do so. "And your Lord is not forgetful." "Verily there is a good example for you in the ways of the Prophet."

83. Narrated by Zaid bin Wahb (ra):

Hudhayfah saw a person who was not performing the bowing and prostrations perfectly. He said to him, "You have not prayed and if you should die you would die on a religion other than that of Muhammad."

84. Narrated by Al-Bara' (ra):

The bowing, the prostrations, the period of standing after bowing and the interval between the two prostrations of the Prophet used to be equal in duration.

85. Narrated by 'Abdullaah bin Malik bin Buhaina (ra):

Whenever the Prophet used to offer prayer he used to keep arms away (from the body) so that the whiteness of his armpits was visible.

86. Narrated by Ibn 'Abbaas (ra):

The Prophet was ordered (by Allaah) to prostrate on seven parts and not to tuck up the clothes or hair (while praying). Those parts are: the forehead (along with the tip of the nose), both hands, both knees, and (toes of) both feet.

87. Narrated by Abu Bakr As-Siddeeq (ra):

I asked Prophet Muhammad (PBUH) to teach me an invocation so that I may invoke Allaah with it in my prayer. He told me to say, *"Allaahumma innee dhalamtu nafsee dhulman katheeran, wa laa yaghfiruth-thunooba illaa anta, faghfir lee maghfiratan min 'indika warhamnee innaka antal-Ghafoorur-Raheem* (O Allaah! I have done great injustice to myself and none except You forgives sins, so please forgive me and be merciful to me as You are the Forgiver, the Merciful)."

88.
Narrated by Umm Salamah (ra):

Whenever Prophet Muhammad (PBUH) finished his prayers with *tasleem*, the women would get up and he would stay on for a while in his place before getting up. Ibn Shihab said, "I think (and Allaah knows better), that the purpose of his stay was that the women might leave before the men who had finished their prayer."

89.
Narrated by Ibn 'Umar (ra):

While 'Umar bin Al-Khattaab was standing and delivering the sermon on a Friday, one of the Companions of the Prophet, who was one of the foremost *Muhaajirs* (emigrants) came. 'Umar said to him, "What is the time now?"
He replied, "I was busy and could not go back to my house till I heard the Adhaan. I did not perform more than the ablution."
Thereupon 'Umar said to him, "Did you perform only the ablution although you know that Prophet Muhammad (PBUH) used to order us to take a bath (on Fridays)?"

90. Narrated by Abu Hurayrah (ra):

He heard Prophet Muhammad (PBUH) saying, "If the prayer has started do not run for it but just walk for it calmly and pray whatever you get, and complete whatever is missed."

91. Narrated by Ibn 'Umar (ra):

One of the wives of 'Umar (bin Al-Khattaab) used to offer the Fajr and the 'Isha prayer in congregation in the mosque. She was asked why she had come out for the prayer as she knew that 'Umar disliked it, and he has great *ghayra* (self-respect). She replied, "What prevents him from stopping me from this act?" The other replied, "The statement of Prophet Muhammad (PBUH): 'Do not stop Allaah's women-slave from going to Allaah's Mosques' prevents him."

92. Narrated by Jaabir bin 'Abdullaah (ra):

The Prophet used to stand by a stem of a date-palm tree (while delivering a sermon). When the pulpit was placed for him we heard that stem crying like a pregnant she-camel till the Prophet got down from the pulpit and placed his hand over it.

93. Narrated by Anas (ra):

While the Prophet was delivering the Khutbah on a Friday, a man stood up and said, "O, Prophet Muhammad (PBUH)! The livestock and the sheep are dying, so pray to Allaah for rain." So he (the Prophet) raised both his hands and invoked Allaah (for it).

94. Narrated by Abu Hurayrah (ra):

Prophet Muhammad (PBUH) talked about Friday and said, "There is an hour (opportune time) on Friday and if a Muslim gets it while praying and asks something from Allaah, then Allaah will definitely meet his demand." And he (the Prophet) pointed out the shortness of that time with his hands.

95. Narrated by Sahl bin Sad (ra):

There was a woman amongst us who had a farm and she used to sow *silq* (a kind of vegetable) on the edges of streams in her farm. On Fridays she used to pull out the *silq* from its roots and put the roots in a utensil. Then she would put a handful of powdered barley over it and cook it. The roots of the *silq* were a substitute for meat. After finishing the Jumu'ah prayer we used to greet her and she would give us that food which we would eat with our hands, and because of that meal, we used to look forward to Friday.

Hadiths from the Book of The Two Festivals (Eids)

96. Narrated by Al-Bara' (ra):

I heard the Prophet (PBUH) delivering a Khutbah saying, "The first thing to be done on this day (first day of 'Eid ul-Adha) is to pray; and after returning from the prayer we slaughter our sacrifices (in the name of Allaah) and whoever does so, he acted according to our Sunnah (traditions)."

97. Narrated by Ibn Abbaas (ra):

The Prophet (PBUH) said, "No good deeds done on other days are superior to those done on these (first ten days of Dhul Hijjah)." Then some Companions of the Prophet said, "Not even Jihad?" He replied, "Not even Jihad, except that of a man who does it by putting himself and his property in danger (for Allaah's Sake) and does not return with any of those things."

98. Narrated by Ibn Abbaas (ra):

I (in my childhood) went out with the Prophet on the day of 'Eid ul-Fitr or 'Eid-ul-Adha. The Prophet prayed and then delivered the Khutbah and then went towards the women, preached and advised them and ordered them to give alms.

Hadiths from the Book of Witr Prayer

99. Narrated by 'Abdullaah bin 'Umar (ra):

The Prophet (PBUH) said, "Night prayer is offered as two *rakaat* followed by two *rakaat* and so on, and if you want to finish it, pray only one *rakah* which will be *witr* for all the previous *rakaat.*" Al-Qasim said, "Since we attained the age of puberty we have seen some people offering a three-*rakaat* prayer as *witr* and all that is permissible. I hope there will be no harm in it."

100. Narrated by 'Aishah (ra):

Prophet Muhammad (PBUH) used to pray eleven *rakaat* at night and that was his night prayer and each of his prostrations lasted for a period enough for one of you to recite fifty verses before Prophet Muhammad (PBUH) raised his head. He also used to pray two *rakaat* (sunnah) before the (compulsory) Fajr prayer and then lie down on his right side till the Mu'adhdhin came to him for the prayer.

Have you bought "SuperCharge Homeschooling's Pre-K & Kindergarten Curriculum"?

Pre-K Curriculum

Kindergarten Curriculum

Have You Bought the Series: "Things Every Kid Should Know: Drugs, Alcohol, Smoking, Bullying and Junk Food" for Your Kids By An "11 Year Old" Author, Alya Nuri?

Have You Bought the Series: "Things Every Kid Should Know: Strangers, Fire and Reduce, Reuse & Recycle" for Your Kids By A "8 Year Old" Author, Zafar Nuri?

Have You Bought the Series: "Things Every Kid Should Know: Hand Washing" for Your Kids By A "6 Year Old" Author, Arsalon Nuri?

Books By Zohra Sarwari

E-books by Zohra Sarwari